PUMPKIN SOUP

by Lori Gardner
Published by Provo Craft
Provo, Utah
Managing Editor, Clella Gustin
Design and Book Coordinator, Barbara Sanderson
Photography by Craig Young

Warehouse orders for this book may be placed at the Provo Craft Warehouse, 1-800-937-7686, 285 East 900 South, Provo, Utah 84606. If you do not have a wholesale account, you may order retail from Provo Craft Shipping Department at 1-800-563-8679, 295 West Center Street, Provo, Utah 84601.

Alternate wood sources are: A & P Craft Supply, 1-800-748-5090, 850 West 200 South, Lindon, Utah 84042, and Hansens' Wood Crafts, 1-801-227-7189, 460 East 1070 South, Orem, Utah 84097.

The cans used in these projects are available at any large paint store.

TABLE OF CONTENTS

Another book and Computer clip-art
by Lori Gardner

Honey Bears
40-6128
wood project book

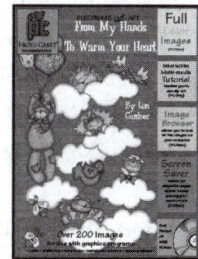

From My Hands To
Warm Your Heart
40-6137
Computer clip-art

GENERAL INSTRUCTIONS

Base: Application of paint to a surface for full opaque coverage. Cover the area with two to three coats of paint evenly and smoothly. It is better to apply several thin coats of paint rather than one heavy coat. Dry and sand lightly between coats.

Wash: Thin the paint with water. This should be a transparent look.

Transferring Pattern: To apply pattern to a project, trace from the original source onto tracing paper. Slip a piece of transfer paper between the tracing and painting surface. With a pencil or stylus, trace essential lines using very light pressure. Unwanted lines can be removed with a kneaded eraser.

Floating: A technique used to apply shading and highlighting. Dampen the largest flat brush that will be accommodated by the area to be floated. Blot the brush on a towel. Load one corner of the brush up to 1/3 of the width of the chisel edge of a flat brush. Stroke the brush back and forth on the palette to work the paint into the bristles and soften the color. Apply the brush to the painting surface. The color should appear strongest at the loaded corner and gradually fade to clear water on the opposite corner. If the paint spreads all the way across the chisel edge, rinse the brush and try again.

One Strokes: These are sometimes referred to as "comma" strokes. Using a small round brush, load the entire brush and stroke in the shape of a "comma".

Spattering: Application of small dots to the painting surface. This resembles fly specks. Wet an old tooth brush and shake or blot off excess water. Dip the end of the bristles in paint. Blot off the excess paint. Hold about 6 to 8 inches away from the project. Point the brush head toward the project and draw a finger or thumb across the bristles toward you causing the paint to spatter away from you. Size of the spatters is in direct relationship to the amount of water used. Using more water causes larger spatters and less water causes smaller spatters.

Dry Brush: To achieve a soft light appearance, load a stipple or fabric brush into paint. Wipe out paint on a paper towel until there is very little left. Holding the brush in a vertical position, apply paint moving from the center of the area to the outside using a circular motion. The color will soften as you move toward the outer edges of the area.

Lori's rubber stamps: I carefully cut out shapes from the end of pencil erasers or from the Pink Pearl eraser using an X-acto knife. (See illustration). I use dry clean sponges (cut from upholstery or camping foam) for my stamp pads. You can also use felt. Pour a tiny amount of paint onto the sponge and work in a little with your paint brush. Dip the stamp onto the pad and press onto the wood. Wa-la!

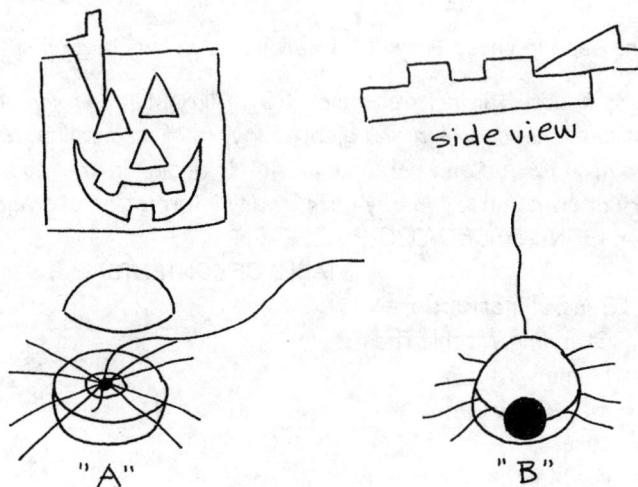

side view

Spiders: Cut 4 pieces of Black Pearl Cotton 2 1/2" long and 1 piece approximately 10" long for the hanging spider. Paint two 5/8" rounded wood plugs Charcoal. Glue them together using hot glue (see illustration A). Cut off a tiny bit of hanging string and glue a tiny black pom pom on for head (see illustration B). You're through!

"A"   "B"

Preparing Cans for Painting and Technique to Apply Paint: This is simple. Spray the "can" with a matte finish white spray paint. I do it outside. You only need one light coat and it doesn't need to cover that well. It gives the "can" a surface that will hold your acrylic paint. To paint with acrylics, you will need 2 to 3 heavy coats to cover. Sponges work well to apply the paint.

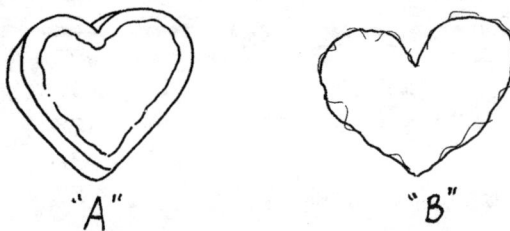

"A"   "B"

Lori's Inking Technique: Begin inking using a .35 Rotring Rapidoliner or other permanent Black pen. Simply ink as shown on the pattern; lines should look unsteady and wiggly (see illustration). Next use a .25 pen and trace (very loosely) around the same line, as shown in the illustration.

HeatnBond Method: Trace exact outline onto paper side of Heat n' Bond and cut out leaving approximately 1/8" excess around the edges. Iron onto wrong side of

heat-n-bond   cut out   FABRIC   cut-out   wood

1   2   3   4   5

fabric and cut out shape exactly on traced lines. Peel off the paper. Using the tip of a hot iron, iron the shape into place directly on the wood, being careful not to touch iron to the wood (see illustration).

STANDING WITCHIE POO
This wood is not available through Provo Craft

PALETTE:
CERAMCOAT BY DELTA

Pumpkin	Dusty Purple	Apple Green	Leaf Green
Charcoal	Medium Flesh	Gypsy Rose	Desert Sun Orange
White	Autumn Brown		

SUPPLIES:
Black Tulle (for accents)
Pink Pearl Eraser (New!) (For cutting out the moon, large star and Jack o' lantern face stamps.)
Black Raffia
Black Pearl Cotton
Tiny Black Pom Pom
Two 5/8" Axle Caps
Two Purple Star Jewels
One Gold Star Jewel
Fabric Scraps (for patches)
HeatnBond

WOOD CUTTING HINTS: Body, hands and boots are cut from 3/4" wood. The brim is cut from 1/4" wood. The broom is a 1/4" dowel 17" long. Two dowels for the arms are 1/2" x 4 1/2" long. Two dowels for the legs are 1/2" x 7 1/2" long. The overall finished wood size is 22 3/4" x 15".

PAINTING INSTRUCTIONS:
1. Medium Flesh: Base in the face.
2. Desert Sun Orange: Shade under the brim area
3. Gypsy Rose: Dry brush the cheeks.
4. White: Base in the tooth.
5. Pumpkin: Base in the dress and the dowel arms.
6. Charcoal: Base in the gloves, hat and brim. Stamp the Jack O' Lantern faces on the dress (see General Instructions). Dot the eyes. Base the axle caps (spider body).
7. Dusty Purple: Base in the boots and the cape.
8. Apple Green: Base the legs. Stamp the moons on the hat and brim. Base the boot buckles.
9. Leaf Green: Base the hat band. Stamp the stars on the legs.
10. Apple Green: Highlight the hat band.

Finish: Sand the edges lightly for a worn look. Following the pattern, ink the details using the technique described in the General Instructions. Fuse the patches to the cape (see General Instructions). Spray all the pieces lightly with several coats of the acrylic matte spray. Glue dowel legs and arms in the holes and glue on the boots and gloves. (Make sure to angle the boots out so the witch will stand.)

Broom: Wash the dowel Autumn Brown. Base in the bottom 6" with Charcoal. Fold a handful of black raffia in half and cut to 8" long. Place the black end of the dowel in the center of the folded raffia and tie with black string. Secure raffia with hot glue. Push the other end of the broom up through the hand and secure with glue. Glue the brim to the hat. Tie tulle around the ankles and wrists. Tie two pieces of tulle into bows and glue one to the neck and the other on the hat behind the brim. Glue the jewels to the bow behind the hat brim. Make the spider according to the General Instructions and tie to the brim of the hat.

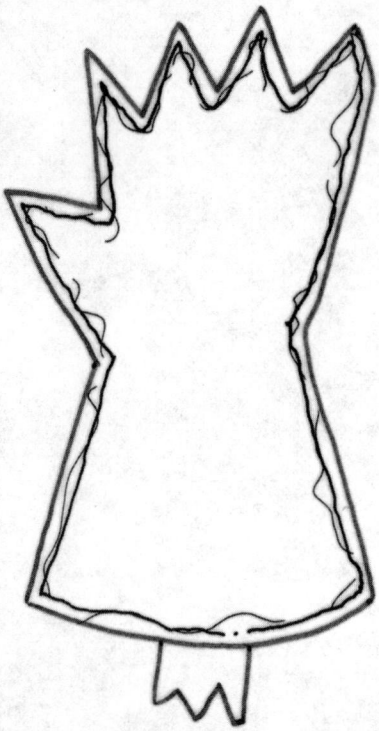
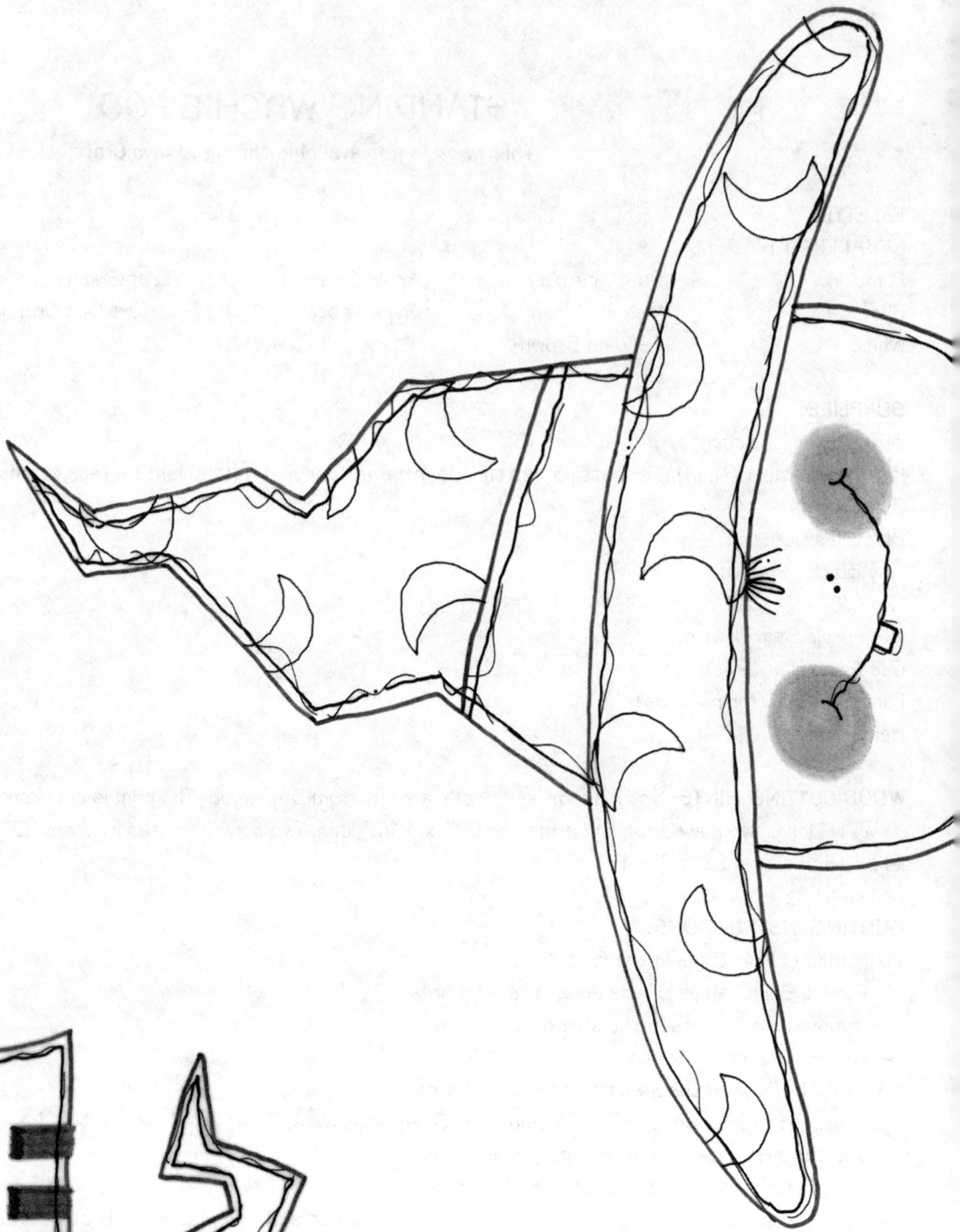
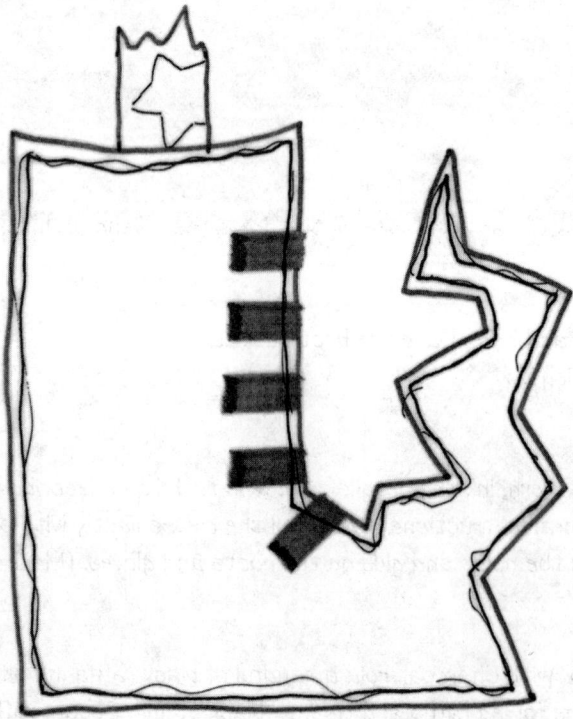

MUMMY YARD STAKE

This wood is not available through Provo Craft

PALETTE:

CERAMCOAT BY DELTA

Sandstone	Dusty Plum	Wedgewood Green
Pale Mint Green	Trail Tan	Territorial Beige
Charcoal	Dark Brown	Stonewedge Green

WOOD CUTTING HINTS: The body and sign are cut from 3/4" pine. The arm with a bear is cut from 1/4" pine. The overall finished size is 10 1/2" x 13".

PAINTING INSTRUCTIONS:

1. Sandstone: Base in the mummy and arm.

2. Trail Tan: Base in the bear.

3. Dusty Plum and Stonewedge Green: Sponge lightly on the mummy and his arm.

4. Wedgewood Green: Base in the patches on the toe and tummy.

5. Stonewedge Green: Shade the mummy. Base in the eye area. Base the sign.

6. Dusty Plum: Base in one patch on the leg.

7. Pale Mint Green: Base in the other patch on the leg.

8. Charcoal: Dot the eyes on the mummy and bear.

9. Dusty Plum and Pale Mint Green: Sponge across the sign lightly. When dry, lightly sand the surface of the sign.

10. Territorial Beige and Pale Mint Green: Sponge lightly on the bear.

11. Territorial Beige: Shade the bear.

12. Dark Brown: Base in the bear's nose.

13. Dusty Plum: Letter the sign.

Finish: Sand all edges lightly for a worn look. Following the pattern, ink details on all the pieces. Assemble the pieces using glue. Spray lightly with acrylic matte spray. Stick this little spook just outside your door. Enjoy!

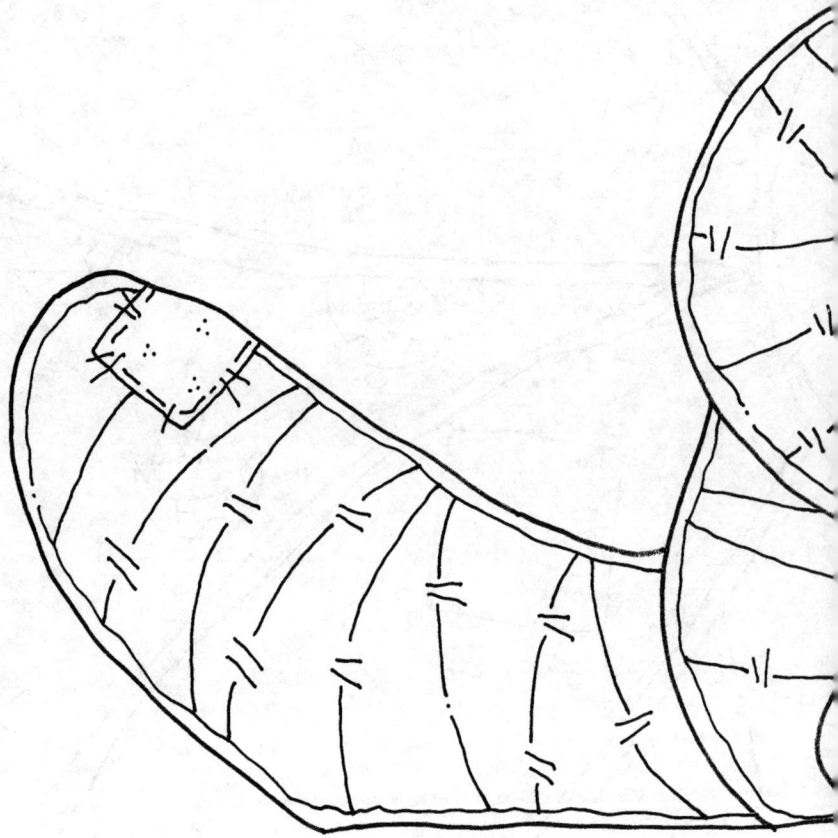

8

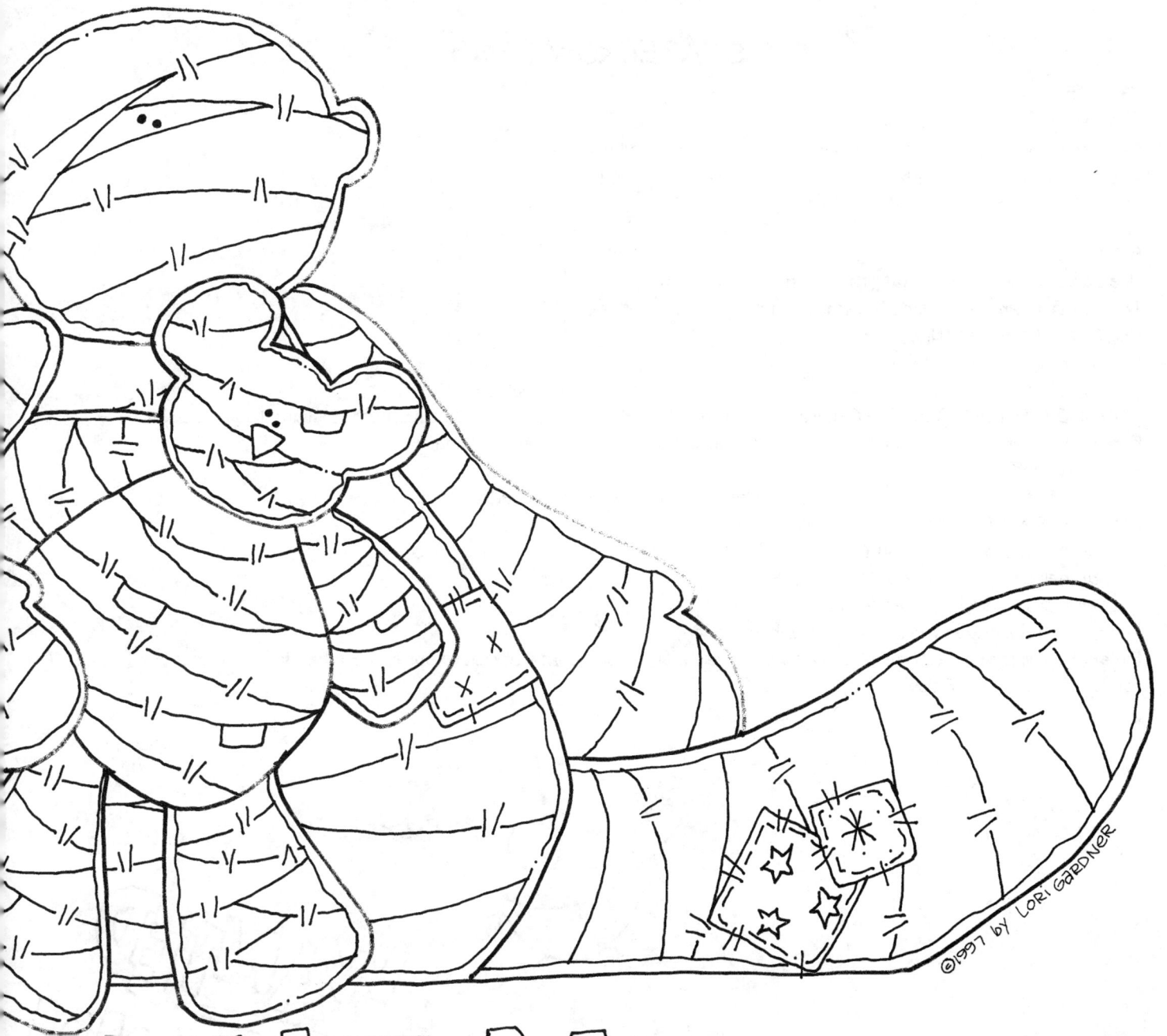

WANT MY
MMY!

©1997 by LORI GARDNER

9

SCARECROW CANS

PALETTE:
CERAMCOAT BY DELTA

Fleshtone	Medium Flesh	Desert Sun Orange
Liberty Blue	Pigskin	Antique White
Charcoal	Queen Anne's Lace	

SUPPLIES:
One Large and One Small Hat (to top off the scarecrows)
Two Red Bandannas (to tie around the cans)
One Gallon Paint Can (New)
One Quart Paint Can (New)

PAINTING INSTRUCTIONS: See General Instructions for preparing cans for painting and technique to apply paint.
Remove the handle from the large can before painting and replace after spraying.
1. Fleshtone: Base in the cans.
2. Queen Anne's Lace/Medium Flesh: Sponge lightly here and there all over the can.
3. Medium Flesh/Fleshtone: Sponge the cheeks.
4. Desert Sun Orange: Base in the mouth. Shade the nose.
5. Charcoal: Stroke the eyes.
6. Liberty Blue: Stroke the lettering.
7. Pigskin and Antique White: Stroke the hair (straw).
Finish: Following the pattern, ink the details. Spray with several coats of matte spray. Tie a bandanna around the "neck".
Top it off with a hat. Enjoy!

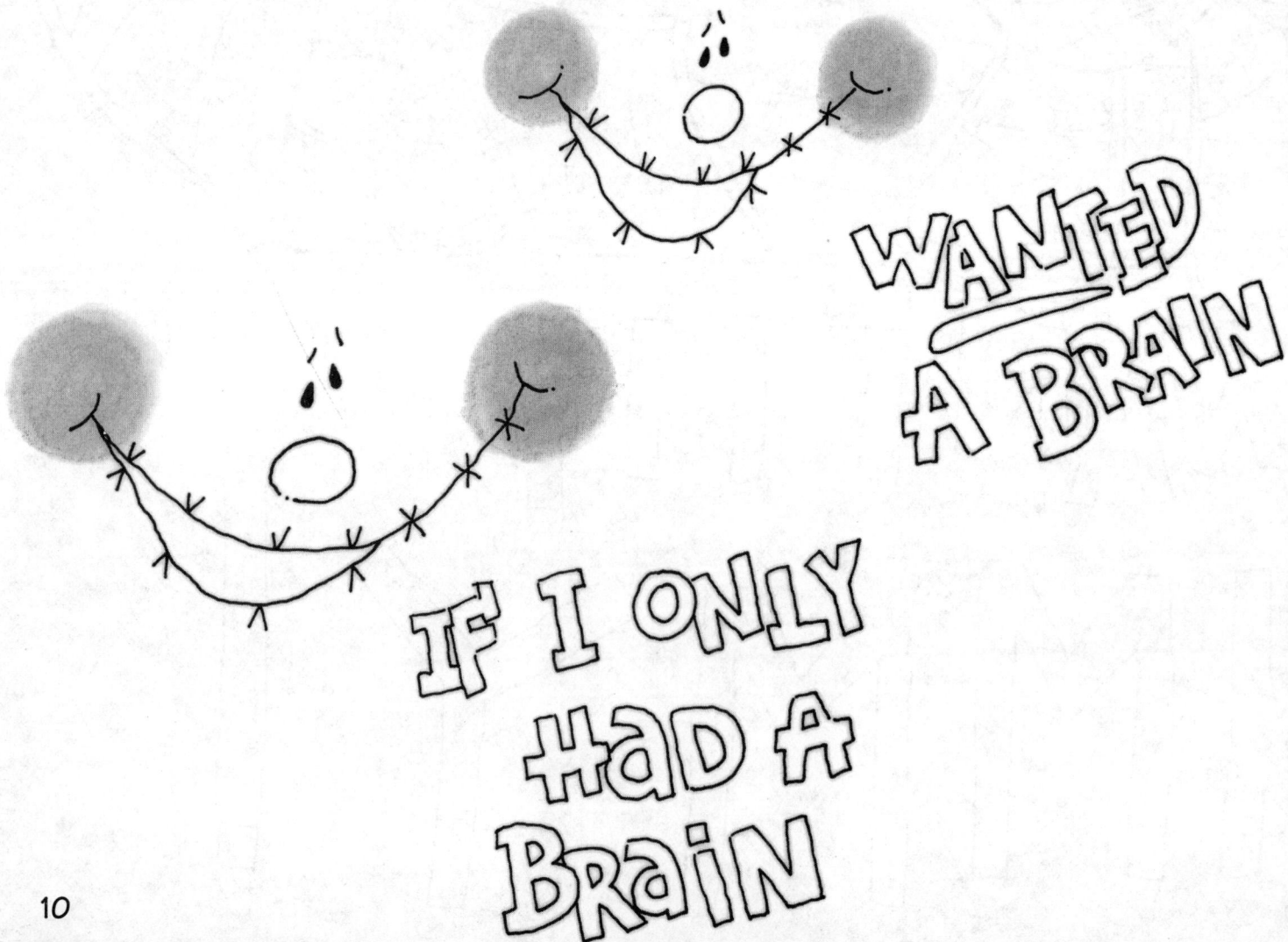

WANTED
A BRAIN

IF I ONLY
HaD A
BRaIN

MICE (all mice)

This wood is not available through Provo Craft

PALETTE:

CERAMCOAT BY DELTA

Gypsy Rose	Trail Tan	Liberty Blue
Charcoal	Mudstone	Autumn Brown
Pumpkin	Cinnamon	

SUPPLIES:

19 Gauge Wire
Black Pearl Cotton
Tiny Mouse-Paper Twist Covered Wire (for arms)
Tiny Black Pom-Pom (for noses on tiny mice)

WOOD CUTTING HINTS: The body, hands, head and feet of the large mice are 3/4" pine. The signs are 1/4" pine. The dowels for the signs are 2 1/2" x 1/8". The dowels for the arms are 3/8" x 6". The two leg dowels for the standing mouse are 3/8" x 3". The two legs for the sitting mouse are 3/8" x 2 1/2" dowels. The noses are 1/2" diameter axle caps. The tiny mice on the pumpkin stack are all 1/4" pine. The legs are 1/8" x 1 1/4" dowels. The overall finished size of the sitting mouse is 11 1/4" x 6 1/4". The standing mouse is 9 1/2" x 9". The finished size of the small mice is approximately 4 1/2" x 3 1/4" depending upon the placement of the arms.

PAINTING INSTRUCTIONS:

1. Mudstone: Base in the dowel legs, arms, heads and bodies.
2. Liberty Blue: Base in the pants.
3. Autumn Brown: Base in the shoes.
4. Trail Tan: Base in the hands.
5. Gypsy Rose: Dry brush the cheeks and ears.
6. Charcoal: Dot the eyes and buttons on the pants. Base the sign stakes and the noses for the large mice.
7. Pumpkin: Base in the signs.
8. Cinnamon: Letter the signs.

Finish - Large Mice: Sand the edges lightly for a worn look. Following the pattern, ink the details using the technique described in the General Instructions. Glue the hands and feet to the dowels and the dowels to the bodies (arm dowel goes through body). For the standing mouse, angle the shoes so he will stand up. Glue the dowels in the signs and in the hands. Glue on the heads and noses. Pull whiskers through the nose and glue in place. Curl wire for tails and glue in place. Spray with several coats of your favorite acrylic matte spray.

Finish - Small Mice on the Pumpkin Stack: Sand edges lightly for a worn look. Following the pattern, ink the details using the technique described in the General Instructions. Assemble mice using glue to secure at all parts. Curl wire and glue in place. Glue on tiny pom-poms for noses and pull whiskers through the nose and glue in place. (Please note that one mouse has no suspenders and his head is glued on upside down. His tail comes out at the center of his pants.) Spray with several light coats of your favorite acrylic matte spray.

oh, Rats!

14

BIG MAN ON CAMPUS (FRANKENSTIEN)

This wood is not available through Provo Craft

PALETTE:

CERAMCOAT BY DELTA

Trail Tan	Cinnamon	Territorial Beige
Wisteria	Charcoal	Dark Brown
White	Dusty Plum	Flesh Tone
Desert Sun Orange	Stonewedge Green	Tangerine
Autumn Brown	Terra Cotta	Silver Gleams

SUPPLIES:

Lori Gardners "Pumpkin Soup" Fabric or any other (Scraps of fabric for "U" and patches)
.35 and .01 Permanent Black Pens (for inking details)
HeatnBond
Two Axle Pegs (painted silver)
Rib Knit Fabric for Socks
19 Gauge Black Wire
Black Pearl Cotton
1/2 Pint Can

WOOD CUTTING HINTS: All pieces are cut from 3/4" wood. Two 1/2" dowels are cut 8 1/2" long. One 1/4" dowel is cut 2 1/2" long. One 1/4" dowel is cut 1 1/4" long. The overall finished size is 32" x 13".

PAINTING INSTRUCTIONS:

1. Flesh Tone: Base in the face, hands and dowel legs.
2. Wisteria and Stonewedge Green: Lightly sponge here and there on the face, hands and legs.
3. Charcoal: Base in the hair and dot the eyes.
4. Desert Sun Orange: Base in the inside of the mouth.
5. White: Base in the tooth.
6. Trail Tan: Base in the shorts.
7. Wisteria: Base in the shirt and sleeves.
8. Tangerine: Base in the sign.
9. Territorial Beige: Base in the boots.
10. Cinnamon: Base wide stripes of plaid on the shorts. Base the heart on the shirt.
    Base the top and bottom borders on the sign.
11. Territorial Beige: Line the thin stripes of the plaid on the shorts. Shade the in seam.
12. Dark Brown: Base the tongue on the boots and shade under the flap on the boots.
    Lightly sponge shadows here and there on the boots.
13. Dusty Plum: Stipple his cheeks.
14. Siver Gleams: Base the bolts.

Finish: Sand the edges lightly for a worn look. Following the pattern, ink details using the technique described in the General Instructions. Dot the lettering using the sharp end of a pencil and dot the shoelace holes on the boots with Charcoal. Trace the "U" onto the paper side of the HeatnBond and cut out leaving approximately 1/8" around the edges. Iron onto the wrong side of fabric and cut out on the traced lines. Peel off the paper and using the tip of a hot iron, iron the "U" in place. Follow the method above to add patches to the sleeves and boots. The hair for the legs: Drill 1/16" holes in the dowels three rows around and an inch apart up and down. Glue the Black Pearl Cotton in the holes as shown and clip 1/2" long. Glue the legs and boots to Frank, making sure to angle the boots so Frank will stand. Wrap the rib knit around the legs for socks and glue in place. Wire the arms to the body and glue the dowel to the sign and in the hand. Glue the Silver "bolts" into holes in the side of his face. Glue the 1 1/4" piece of 1/4" dowel into holes in the back of his head and the front of his body so that his head is raised approximately 1/2" from his body. Spray with several coats of your favorite matte acrylic finish spray. You won't be able to resist this man's goofy little expression at Halloween. Candle Bucket in his hand: Prepare the can for painting (see general instructions). I used a one-half pint can from the paint store. (You could use a tomato sauce can.) Sponge a heavy coat of Cinnamon and let dry. Sponge Autumn Brown and Terra Cotta lightly all over the can. Punch holes all over the can and three in a triangle for eyes and nose. Paint the Jack-O-Lantern face using Charcoal. Spray with acrylic spray. Punch holes for the handle and wire the can to Frank's hand.

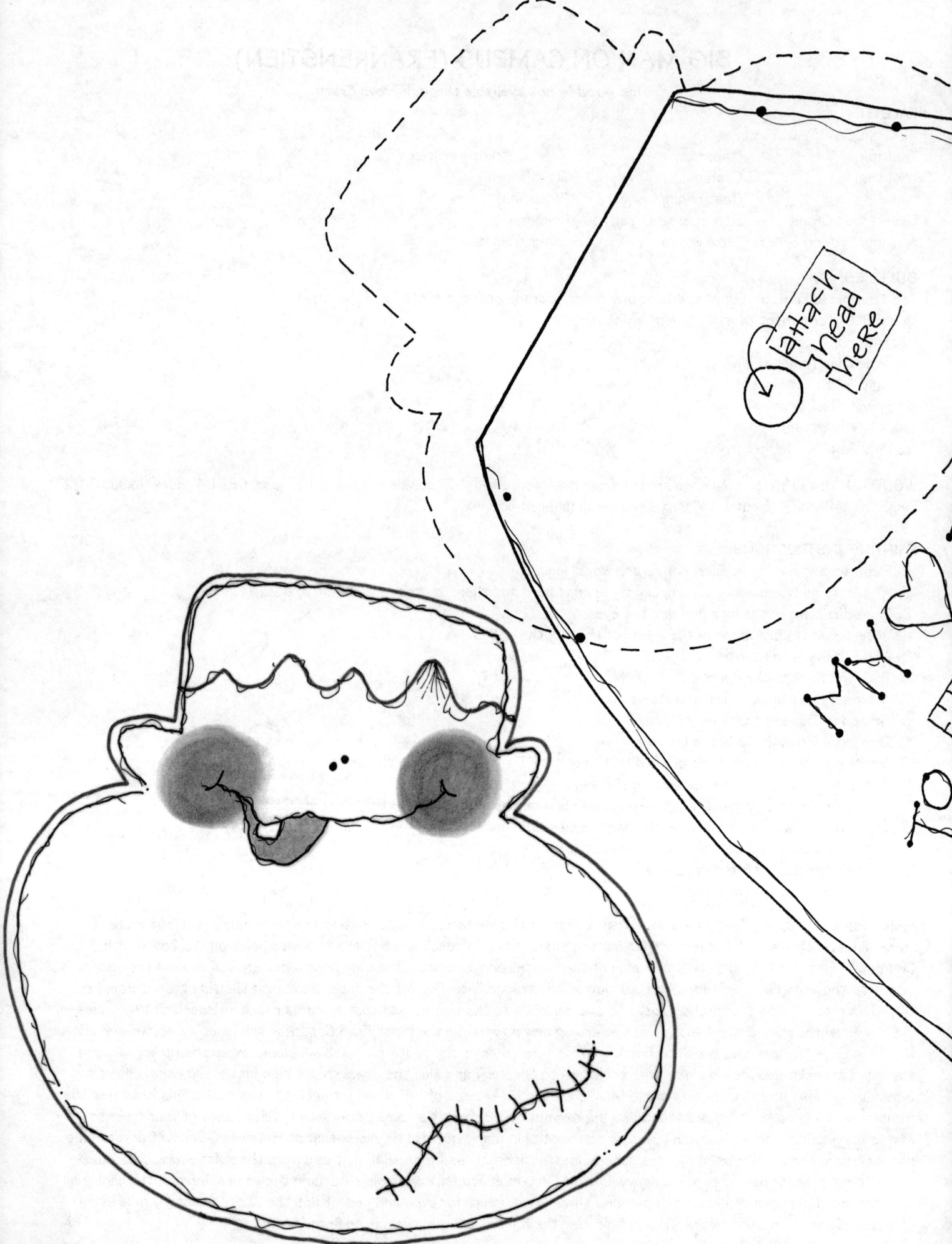

attach
head
heRe

MY

TO

16

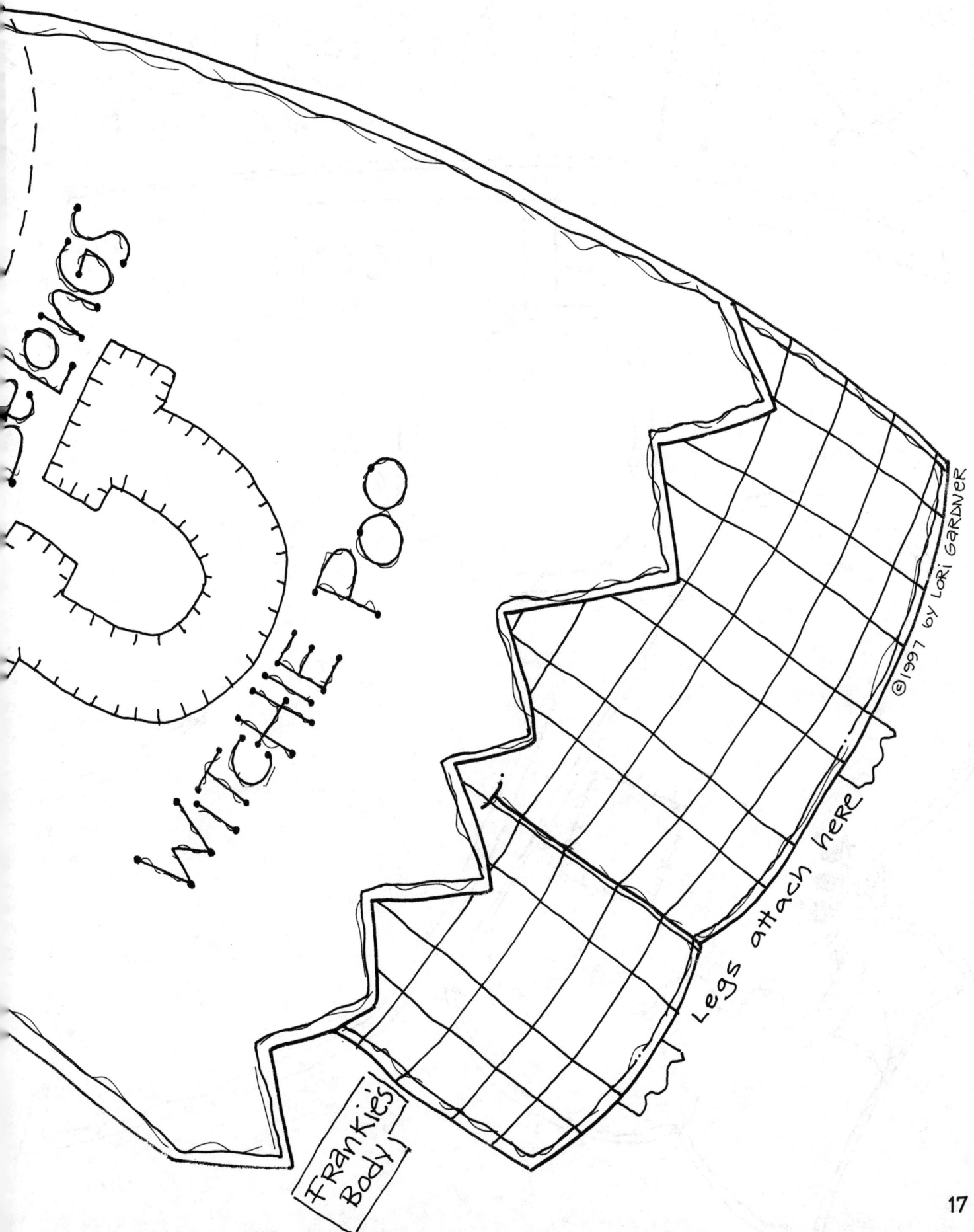

legs

Witchie Poo

Legs attach here

Frankie's Body

Happy Halloweenie!

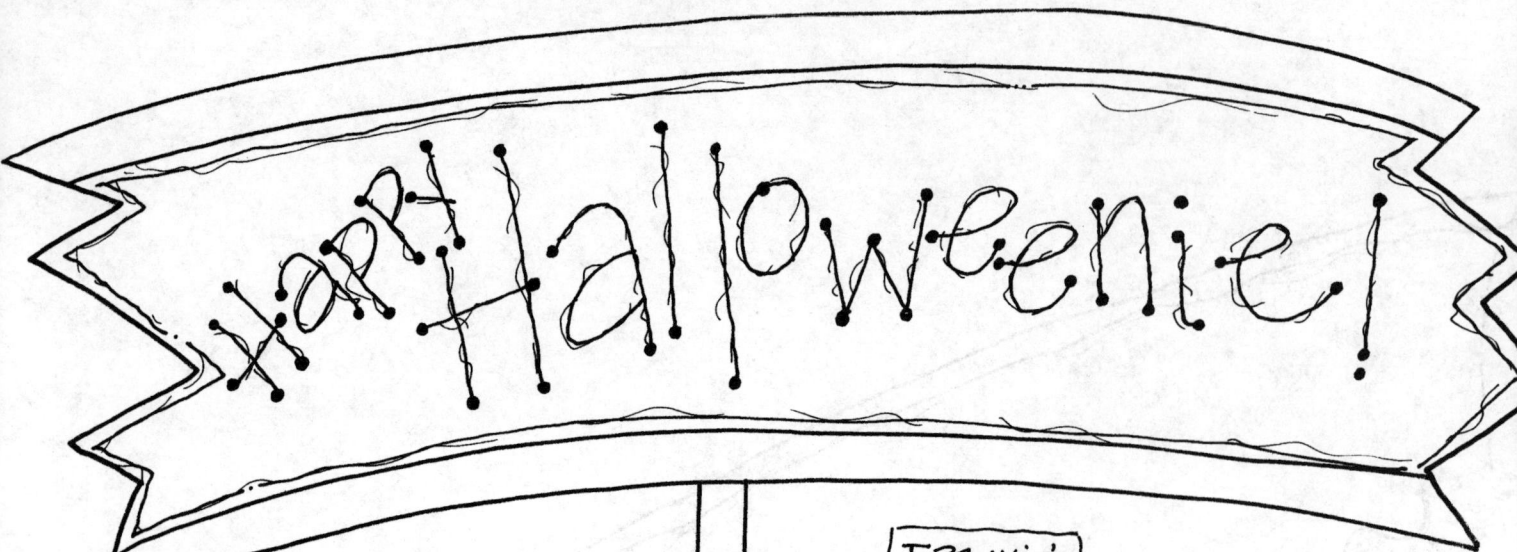

Frankie's Left Arm

Frankie's Boot

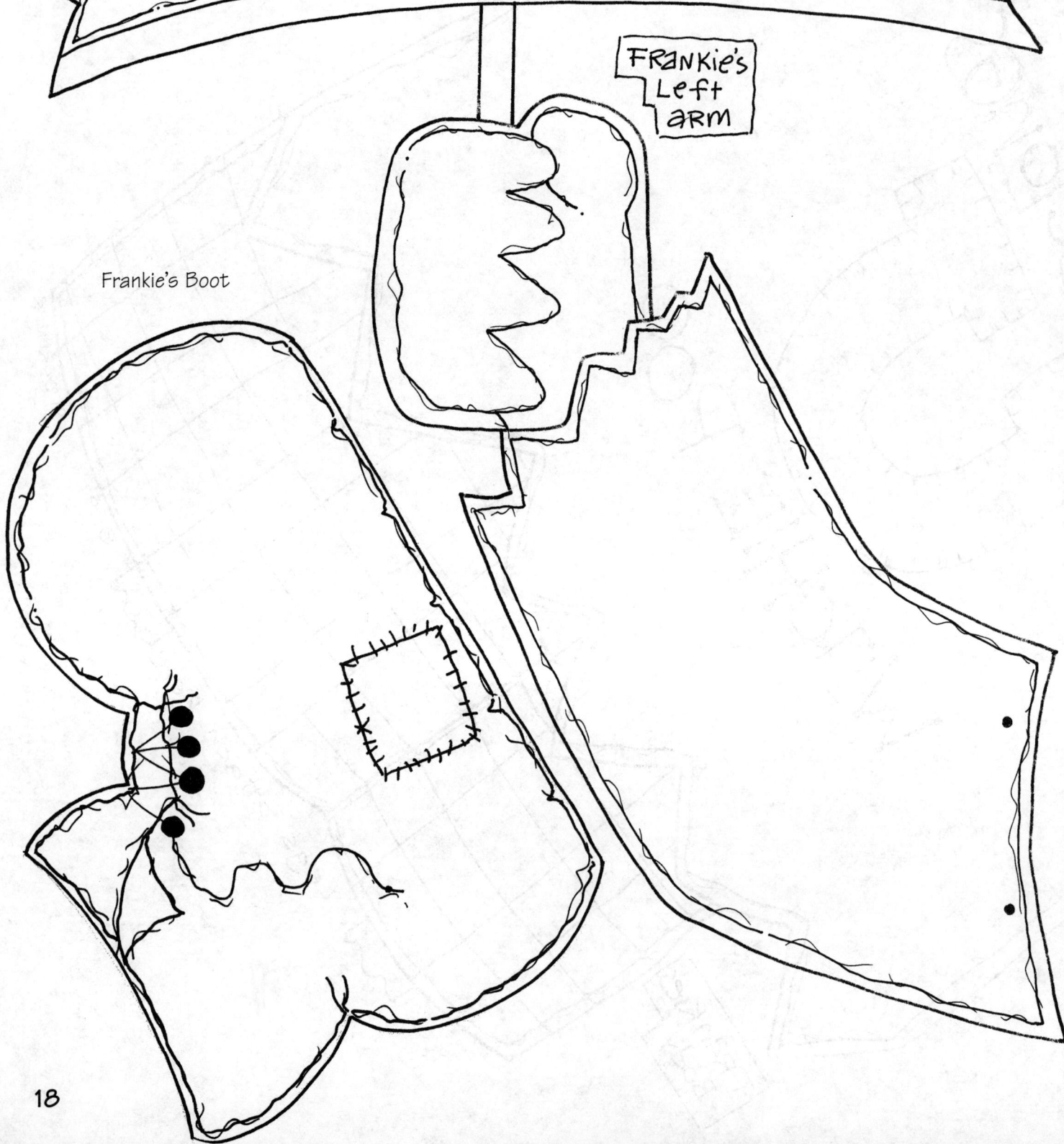

Frankie's Boot

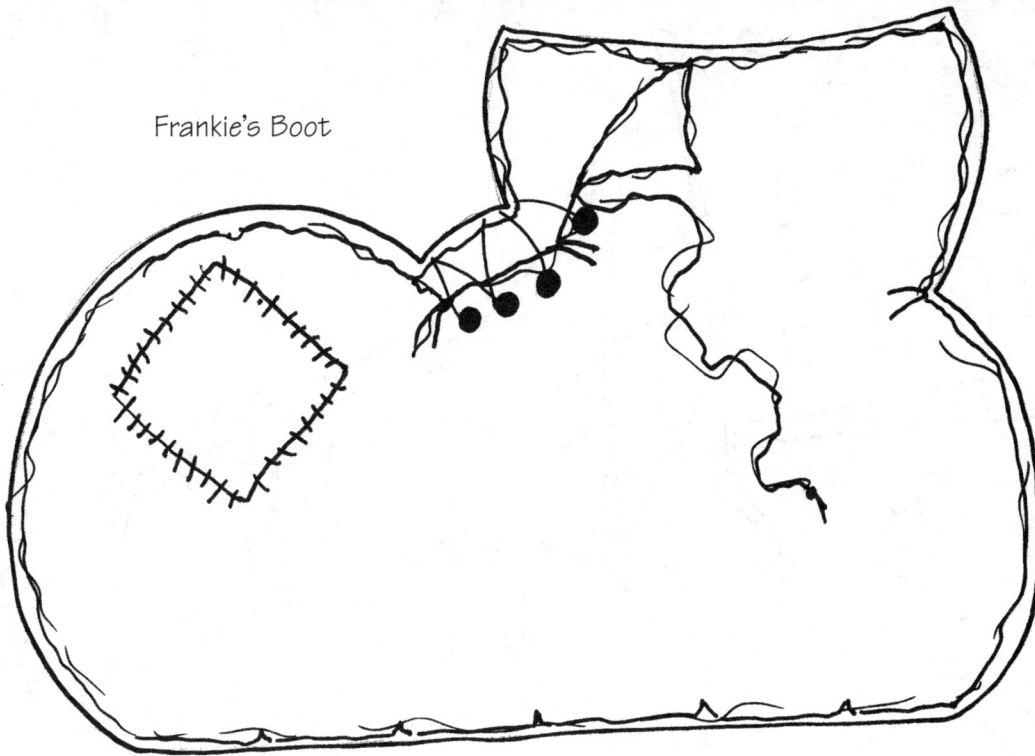

"MUMMY STANDING"

This wood is not available through Provo Craft

PALETTE:
CERAMCOAT BY DELTA

Ocean Mist Blue	Sandstone	Wisteria
Stonewedge Green	Pale Mint Green	Lichen Grey
Territorial Beige	Dark Brown	Charcoal

Mummy's Boot

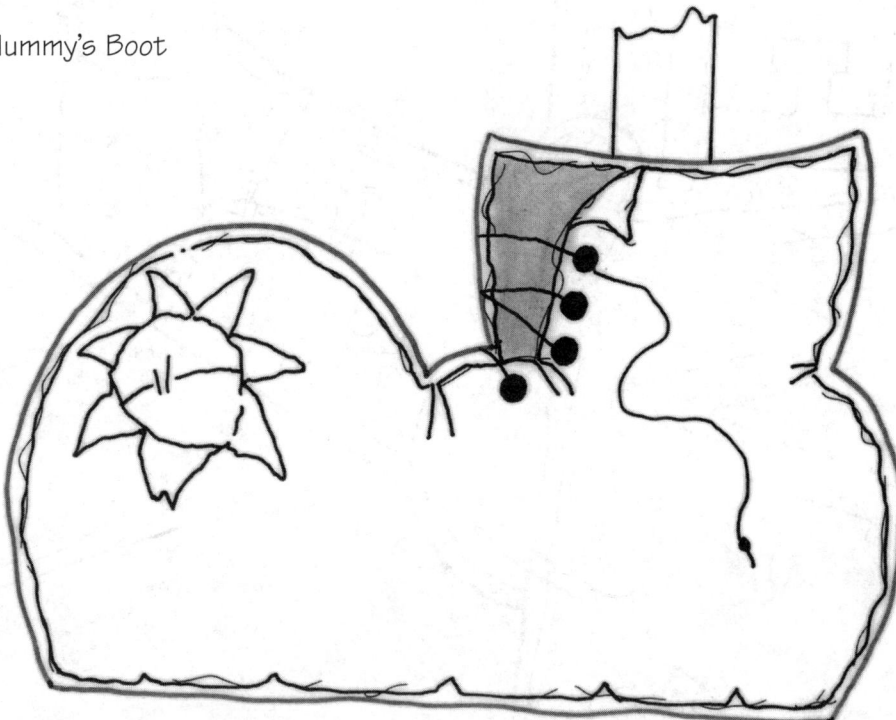

Reverse this pattern
for his other foot and
delete the worn toe.

19

SPOOKS

WELCOME HOME

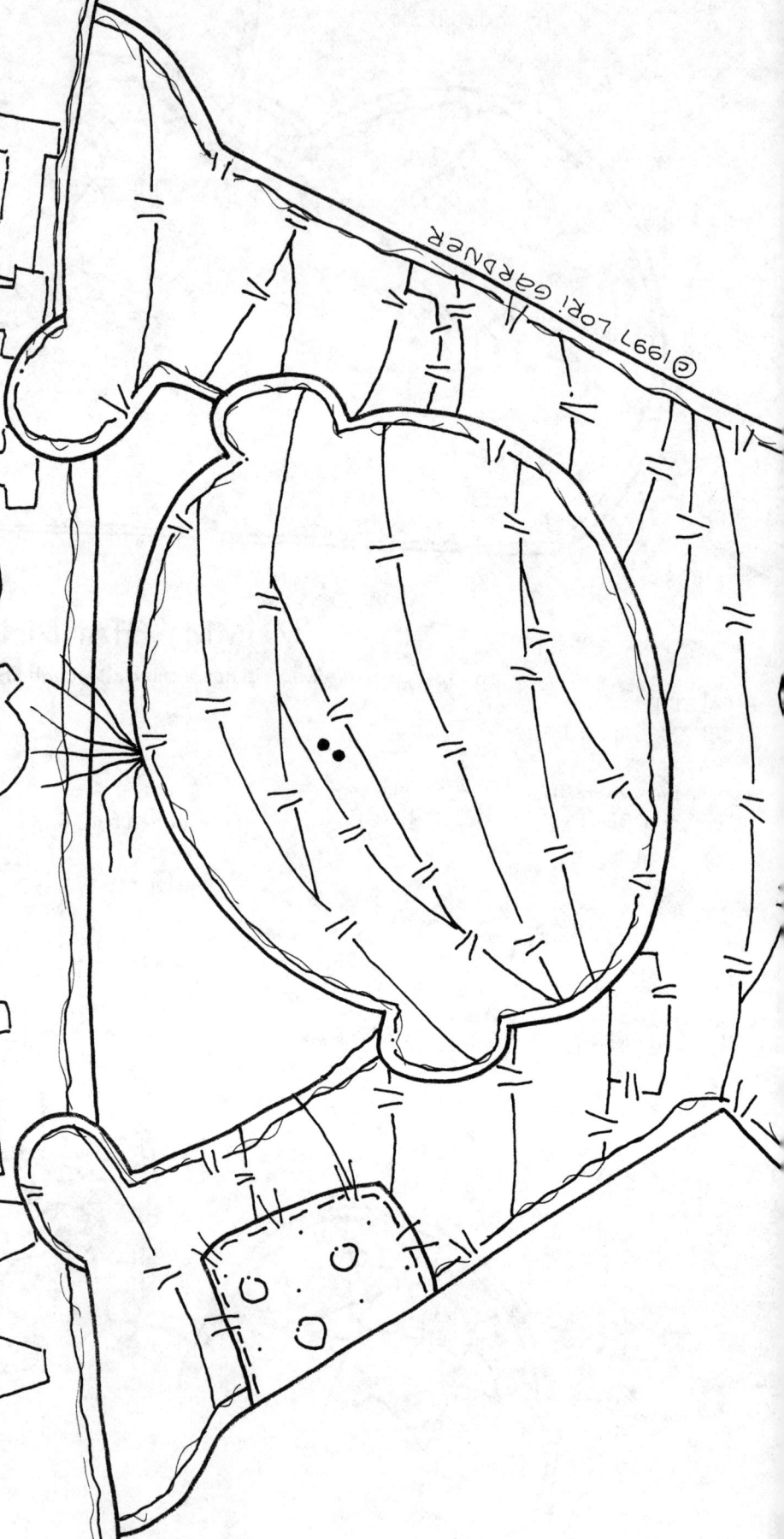

20

SUPPLIES:
Two Strips of Ripped Muslin 1" Wide x 36" Long (for legs)
Old Pair of Socks (for mummy socks)
Black Pearl Cotton

WOOD CUTTING HINTS: All pieces are cut from 3/4" wood. Two dowels are 1/2" x 7 1/2" long for the legs. The overall finished size is 23" x 11 1/2".

PAINTING INSTRUCTIONS:

1. Sandstone: Base in the head, body and dowel legs.
2. Wisteria and Stonewedge Green: Lightly sponge on head, body and legs.
3. Ocean Mist Blue: Base in the patch on the arm.

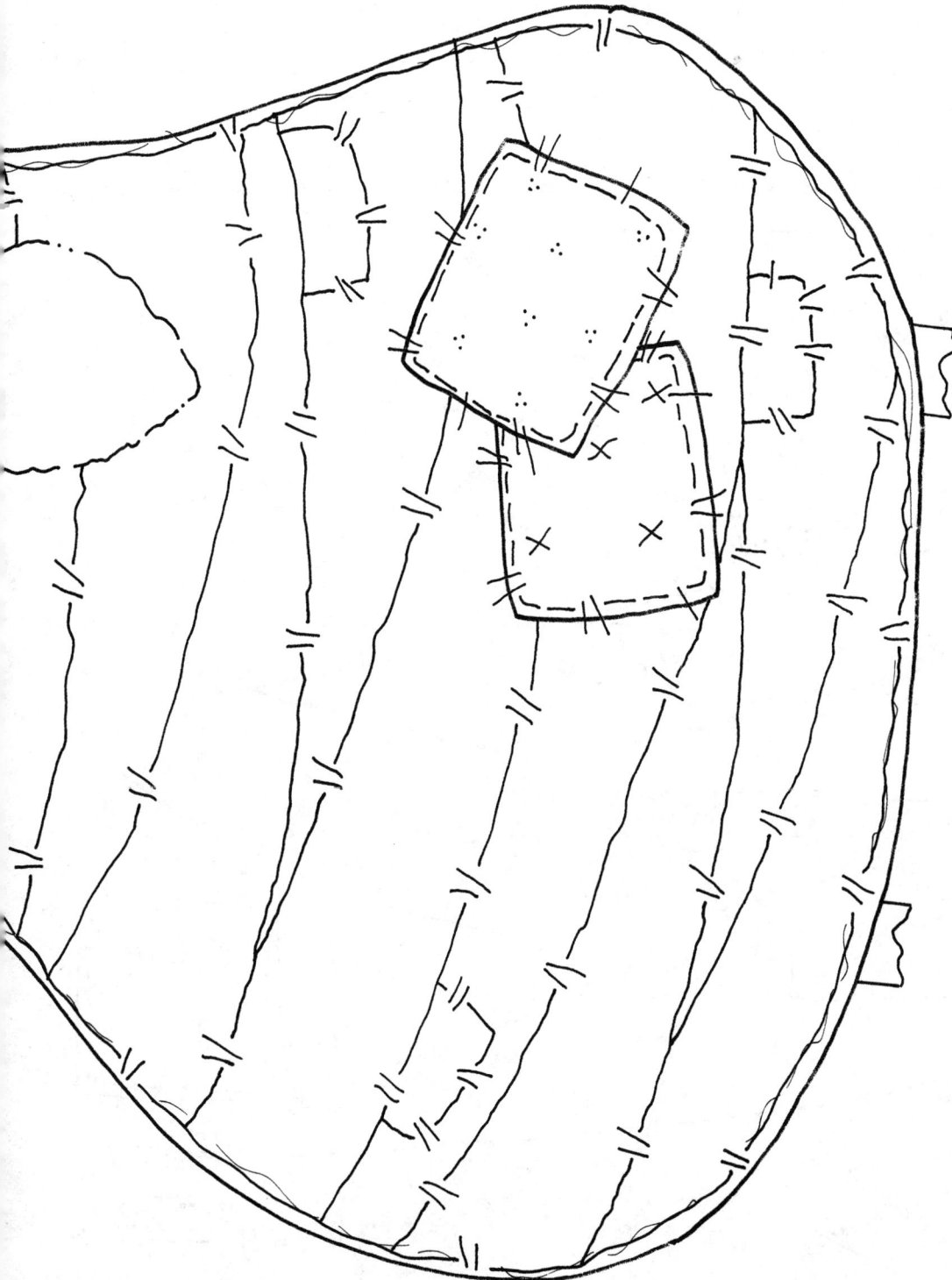

4. Pale Mint Green and Lichen Grey: Base in the two patches on the body.
5. Stonewedge Green: Shade the heart on the body. Base in the eye area on the face. Base in the sign.
6. Territorial Beige: Base in the boots.
7. Dark Brown: Base in the tongue and shade around the flaps on the boots. Base the worn pieces of the boot around the toe. Sponge shading here and there on the boots.
8. Sandstone: Base the toe on one boot.
9. Pale Mint Green and Wisteria: Using a sponge, drag these two paints over the sign surface.
10. Charcoal: Dot the eyes and the holes for the boot laces.
11. Wisteria: Base the letters on the sign.

Finish: Sand the edges of all pieces lightly for a worn look. Following the pattern, ink the details using technique described in the General Instructions. Assemble all the pieces using glue to secure. When gluing on the boots, make sure to angle them so the mummy will stand. Wrap strips of muslin around the mummy's legs and tie knots to hold muslin in place. Wrap the bottom of the legs with pieces of the old socks for his socks. Glue them in place. Cut pieces of Pearl Cotton about 1" long and glue them in a hole on top of his head. What a guy!

MUMMY CAN

PALETTE:
CERAMCOAT BY DELTA

Stonewedge Green	Dusty Plum	Pale Mint Green	Ocean Mist Blue
Lichen Grey	Charcoal	Sandstone	

SUPPLIES:
One Gallon Paint Can (New)

PAINTING INSTRUCTIONS: See the General Instructions for preparing the cans for painting and technique to apply paint. Remove the handle before painting and replace after spraying.

1. Sandstone: Base in the can.
2. Stonewedge Green and Dusty Plum: Sponge lightly here and there all over the can.
3. Stonewedge Green: Base in the eye area.
4. Pale Mint Green: Base in the bottom left patch.
5. Ocean Mist Blue: Base in the top patch.
6. Lichen Grey: Base in the remaining patch.
7. Charcoal: Dot the eyes.

Finish: Following the pattern, ink the details. Spray with several coats of acrylic matte spray. Great for little spooks on Halloween night.

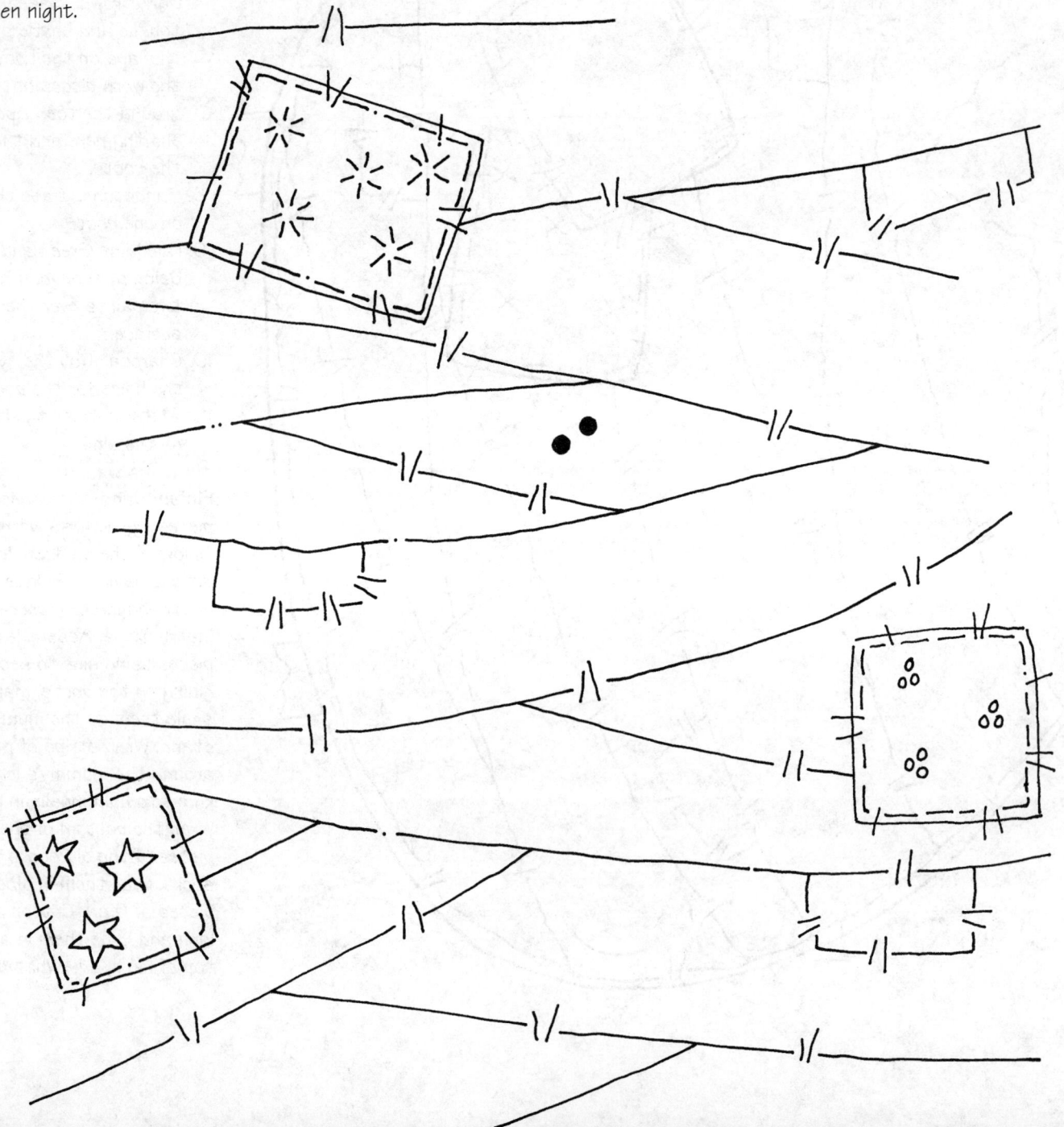

FRANKIE CAN

PALETTE:
CERAMCOAT BY DELTA

Stonewedge Green	Pale Mint Green	Wisteria
Charcoal	Silver Gleams	White

SUPPLIES:
One Gallon Paint Can (New)

PAINTING INSTRUCTIONS: See General Instructions for preparing cans for painting and technique to apply paint. Remove the handle before painting and replace after spraying.

1. Stonewedge Green: Base in the can.
2. Pale Mint Green and Wisteria: Sponge lightly here and there on the entire can.
3. Wisteria: Sponge on the cheeks. Base in the mouth.
4. Pale Mint Green: Base in the lettering.
5. Charcoal: Base in the hair all around the can. Dot the eyes.
6. Gleams - Silver: Base the "ears" (handle holders).
7. White: Base the tooth.

Finish: Following the pattern, ink details. Spray with several coats of acrylic matte spray. Great for holding a candle or fill with treats. My kids use them for trick or treating.

PUMPKIN TRICK OR TREAT CAN

PALETTE:
CERAMCOAT BY DELTA

Calypso Orange	Tangerine	Dark Goldenrod
Pumpkin	Leaf Green	Apple Green
White	Charcoal	

SUPPLIES:
One Gallon Paint Can (New)
New Eraser (for moon cut out for stamping)
X-acto Knife (see general instructions for "cutting stamps")

PAINTING INSTRUCTIONS: See General Instructions for preparing cans for painting and technique to apply paint. Remove the handle before painting and replace after spraying.
1. Calypso Orange: Base in the can.
2. Dark Goldenrod: Stamp the moons all over the can. Base in the mouth.
3. Leaf Green and Apple Green: Stroke in the leaf and vines.
4. Pumpkin and Calypso Orange: Mix on the sponge and sponge on the cheeks.
5. Tangerine: Stroke the lettering.
6. White: Base in the tooth.
7. Charcoal: Dot the eyes.

Finish: Following the pattern, ink details. Spray with several coats of acrylic matte spray. Go trick or treating! Fill with lots of chocolate.

LARGE PUMPKIN SOUP CAN

PALETTE:
CERAMCOAT BY DELTA

Pumpkin	Tangerine	White
Charcoal	Leaf Green	Apple Green

SUPPLIES:
One Gallon Paint Can (New)
New Pink Pearl Eraser (to cut out the swirl shape for stamping
X-acto Knife (see general instructions for "cutting" stamps)

PAINTING INSTRUCTIONS: See the General Instructions for preparing cans for painting and technique to apply paint. Remove the handle before painting and replace after spraying.
1. Pumpkin: Base in the can and lid.
2. Tangerine: Stamp the swirls all over the can as shown in the picture.
3. Tangerine/Pumpkin: Sponge on the cheeks.
4. Leaf Green and Apple Green: Stroke in the leaves and vines.
5. Tangerine: Base in the mouth.
6. White: Base in the teeth.
7. Charcoal: Dot the eyes.

Finish: Following the pattern, ink the details. Spray with several coats of acrylic matte spray. Great for treats. Don't you love my funny poem?

Kats That Hula-Hoop – Frogs & Bats with

MIDDLE PUMPKIN SOUP CAN

PALETTE:
CERAMCOAT BY DELTA

Tangerine	Calypso Orange	Apple Green
White	Bittersweet	Leaf Green
Charcoal		

SUPPLIES:
One (New) Quart Size Paint Can
New Pink Pearl Eraser (to cut out the flower stamp)
X-acto Knife (see general instructions for "cutting" stamps)

PAINTING INSTRUCTIONS: See the General Instructions for preparing cans for painting and technique to apply paint.
1. Bittersweet: Base in the can and lid.
2. Calypso Orange: Stamp the flower all over the can as shown.
3. Tangerine/Bittersweet: Sponge the cheeks.
4. Tangerine: Base in the mouth and nose.
5. White: Base in the teeth.
6. Charcoal: Dot the eyes.
7. Apple Green and Leaf Green: Stroke in the leaf and vines.

Finish: Following the pattern, ink the details. Spray with several coats of acrylic matte spray. Stack on top of the gallon size can. Have Fun!

Kitty Kats that hula-hoop-

Frogs & Bats with Stinky Foot

-Witchies Hat & Grannys Boot - all go in my Pumpkin Soup

FOOT. Witchies Hat & Grannys Boot - all go in

PINT PUMPKIN SOUP CAN

PALETTE:
CERAMCOAT BY DELTA
Pumpkin   Calypso Orange
Bittersweet   Leaf Green
Apple Green   White
Charcoal

SUPPLIES:
One Pint Paint Can (New)
New Pink Pearl Eraser (to cut out the star shape for stamping)
X-acto Knife (see General Instructions for "cutting" the star stamp)

PAINTING INSTRUCTIONS: See General Instructions for preparing the cans for painting and technique to apply paint.
1. Calypso Orange: Base in the can and lid.
2. Bittersweet: Stamp the stars all over the can as shown.
3. Pumpkin/Calypso Orange: Sponge on the cheeks.
4. White: Base in the teeth.
5. Charcoal: Dot the eyes.
6. Leaf Green and Apple Green: Stroke the leaf and vines.
Finish: Following the pattern, ink the details. Spray with several coats of acrylic matte spray. Top off the Pumpkin Soup stack.
Also great for gifts - just fill it with candy and wrap in clear cellophane!

Soup!

kitty kats that hula-hoop-Frogs &

SITTING WITCHIE POO

This wood is not available through Provo Craft

PALETTE:
CERAMCOAT BY DELTA

Tangerine	Ivory	Black
White	Medium Flesh	Leaf Green
Seminole Green	Eggplant	Wisteria
Dusty Plum	Apple Green	Desert Sun Orange
Gypsy Rose		

SUPPLIES:
3 New Pencils with Erasers (cut out a cross and moon and use the other eraser end as is for stamping the dots on the hat)
Black Pearl Cotton
Tiny Black Pom Pom
Two Gold Star Jewels
One Purple Star Jewel
Two 1/2" Diameter Axle Caps
Fabric Scraps (for patches on the dress)
HeatnBond
Black Sparkle Tulle

WOOD CUTTING HINTS: Boots, hands, head and body are cut from 3/4" wood. The brim and sign are cut from 1/4" wood. Two 1/2" dowels 4 1/2" long are cut for the legs. The overall finished size is 13" x 18".

PAINTING INSTRUCTIONS:

1. Medium Flesh: Base in the face and hands.

2. Desert Sun Orange: Shade the face under the brim area and the top of the hands.

3. Gypsy Rose: Dry brush the cheeks.

4. White: Base in the tooth.

5. Wisteria: Base in the dress bottom and the sign.

6. Dusty Plum: Line the stripe on the dress bottom and lettering on the sign.

7. Eggplant: Base the hat, brim and the dress top.

8. Tangerine: Base in the boots.

9. Leaf Green: Base in the hat band and the dowel legs.

10. Ivory: Stamp the moons on the boots.

11. Apple Green: Stamp the "cross" on the legs.

12. Wisteria: Stamp the circle on the hat and brim.

13. Black: Base the boot buckles. Dot the eyes. Base the axle caps (spider's body)

14. Seminole Green: Base 1/4" checks here and there on the hat band and float shade on the band just above the brim area.

Finish: Sand the edges lightly for a worn look. Following the pattern, ink the details using the technique described in the General Instructions. Spray all pieces lightly using acrylic matte spray. Assemble all the pieces using glue to secure. Hang the spider from the hat. (See the General Instructions for making the spider.) Fuse the patches to the dress (see the General Instructions). Tie tulle to the ankles. Tie two bows of tulle and glue one at the neck and the other behind the hat brim. Glue the jewels on the bow behind the brim. This witch looks great on a shelf or over a door.

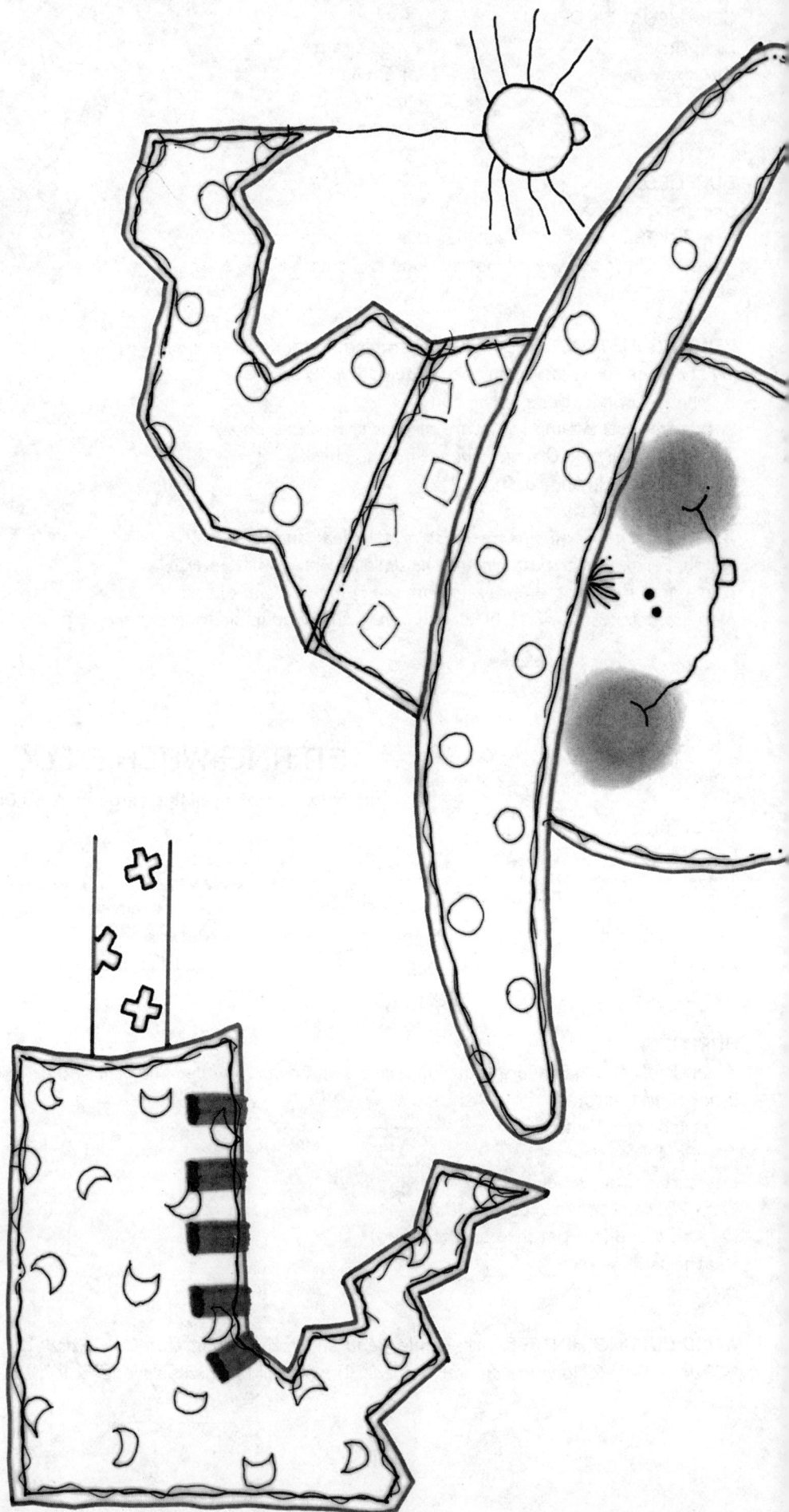

28

Old Witch Lives Here!

WITCHIE POO YARD STAKE

This wood is not available through Provo Craft

PALETTE:

CERAMCOAT BY DELTA

Medium Flesh	White	Black
Charcoal	Eggplant	Wisteria
Apple Green	Gypsy Rose	Desert Sun Orange
Seminole Green	Stonewedge Green	

SUPPLIES:

Black Pearl Cotton
Tiny Black Pom Pom
Pink Pearl Eraser (to cut out star for stamping)
X-acto Knife
Black Tulle 4" x 8"
Scraps of fabric to "fuse" on patches. (I used patches off my new "Pumpkin Soup" fabrics.)
Two 5/8" in diameter Axle Caps (for the spider)

BEWARE of WITCH

WOOD CUTTING HINTS: Head, hat, hands and sign are cut from 3/4" pine. The hat brim is cut from 1/4" pine. The stake is cut from 3/4" wood 36" long. The overall finished size of the project not including the stake is 14" x 8 1/2".

PAINTING INSTRUCTIONS:
1. Wisteria: Base the sign.
2. Medium Flesh: Base in the face and hands.
3. Desert Sun Orange: Shade the tops of the hands and under the brim on the face.
4. Gypsy Rose: Dry brush the cheeks.
5. Black: Dot the eyes.
6. Stonewedge Green: Line the lettering on the sign.
7. Eggplant: Base in the hat and brim.
8. Wisteria: Stamp the stars on the hat and brim.
9. Apple Green: Base in the hat band.
10. Seminole Green: Line the stripes on the hat band.
11. White: Base in the tooth on the face.
12. Charcoal: Base in the spider body (two axle caps).
13. Stake: The stake can be left just sealed or finished as desired.

FINISH: Sand the edges lightly for a worn look. Following the pattern, ink details using the technique described in the General Instructions. Make the spider according to the General Instructions and tie it to the top of the hat. "Spray" all the pieces with acrylic matte spray. "Fuse" the patches to the sign (see General Instructions). Glue the head and hands to the sign and the brim to the hat. Glue a bow of black tulle to the sign just below the face. Attach the sign to a stake. Put the sign out front to ward off evil little spooks or use as a warning to husbands on a bad day!

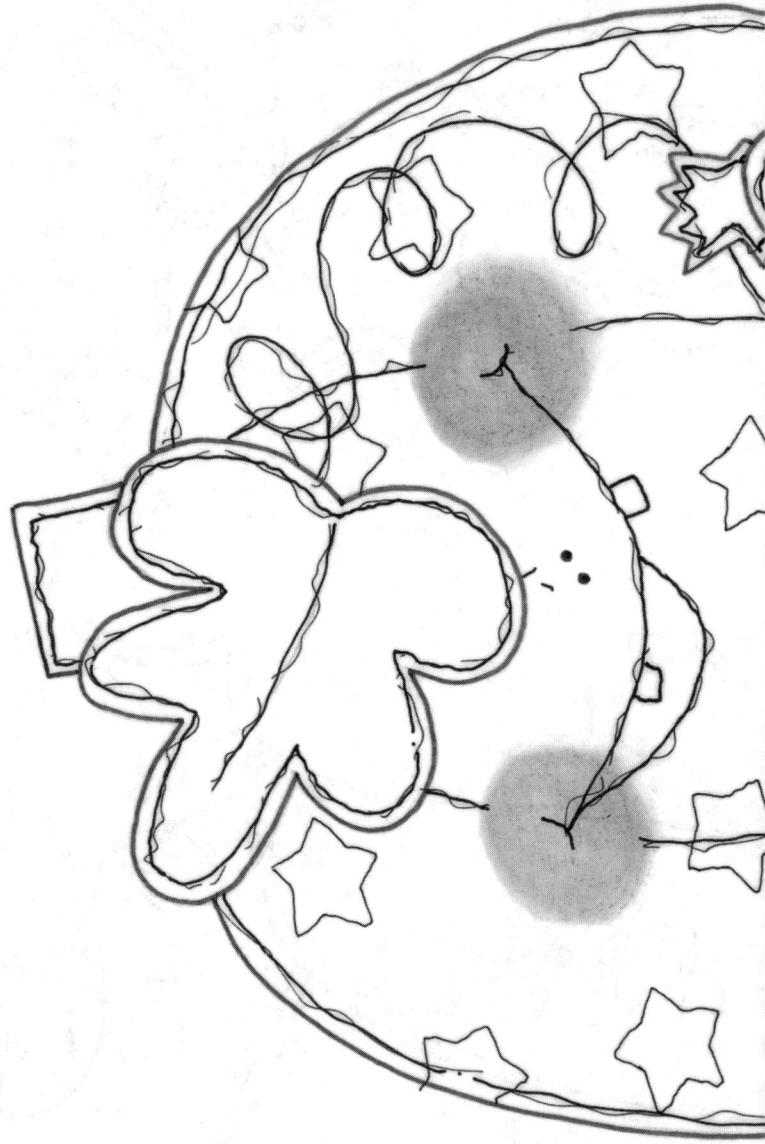

PUMPKIN STACK

PALETTE:

CERAMCOAT BY DELTA

Calypso Orange	Pumpkin
Leaf Green	Apple Green
White	Charcoal
Autumn Brown	Tangerine
Cinnamon	Western Sunset Yellow

WOOD CUTTING HINTS: The pumpkin and base are cut from 3/4" pine. The leaves and all pieces on the mice are 1/4" pine.

SUPPLIES:
Pink Pearl Eraser (New) (to cut out star, flower and curly shapes)
X-acto Knife

PAINTING INSTRUCTIONS: (The instructions for the mice on these pumpkins are on page 12)
1. Calypso Orange: Base in the top pumpkin.
2. Pumpkin: Base in the middle pumpkin and the mouth on the top pumpkin.
3. Tangerine: Base in the bottom pumpkin and the mouth and nose on the middle pumpkin.
4. Western Sunset Yellow: Stamp stars on the top pumpkin.
5. Calypso Orange: Stamp curly shapes on the middle pumpkin.
6. Pumpkin: Stamp flowers on the bottom pumpkin.
7. White: Base in the teeth on all pumpkins.

PART "A"

PART "B"

8. Leaf Green: Base in all the leaves and the base.
9. Leaf Green/Apple Green: Load round liner with Apple Green and dip into the Leaf Green and line the vines.
10. Cinnamon: Dry brush all the cheeks.
11. Charcoal: Dot all the eyes.
12. Apple Green: Paint the base.
13. Autumn Brown: Base the stem on the top pumpkin.

Finish: Sand lightly for a worn look. Following the pattern, ink the details using the technique described in the General Instructions. Spray all pieces with matte acrylic spray. Glue all pieces together as shown.

OVERALLS CAN

PALETTE:
CERAMCOAT BY DELTA
Opaque Red   Liberty Blue   White   Nightfall

SUPPLIES:
One Gallon Paint Can (New)
Two White Buttons (tie with white string)
One Stencil with 1/4" circles (design from Provo Craft #41-5089)

PAINTING INSTRUCTIONS: See the General Instructions for preparing cans for painting and technique to apply paint. Remove the handle before painting and replace after spraying.
1. Opaque Red: Base in the top 2" around the can. Base in the lid.
2. White: Stencil circles around the top 2" of the can.
3. Liberty Blue: Base in the rest of the can and suspenders.
4. Nightfall: Shade around the pocket and under the suspenders.
5. White: Line the stitches.

Finish: Spray with several coats of acrylic matte spray. Glue on buttons. Enjoy!

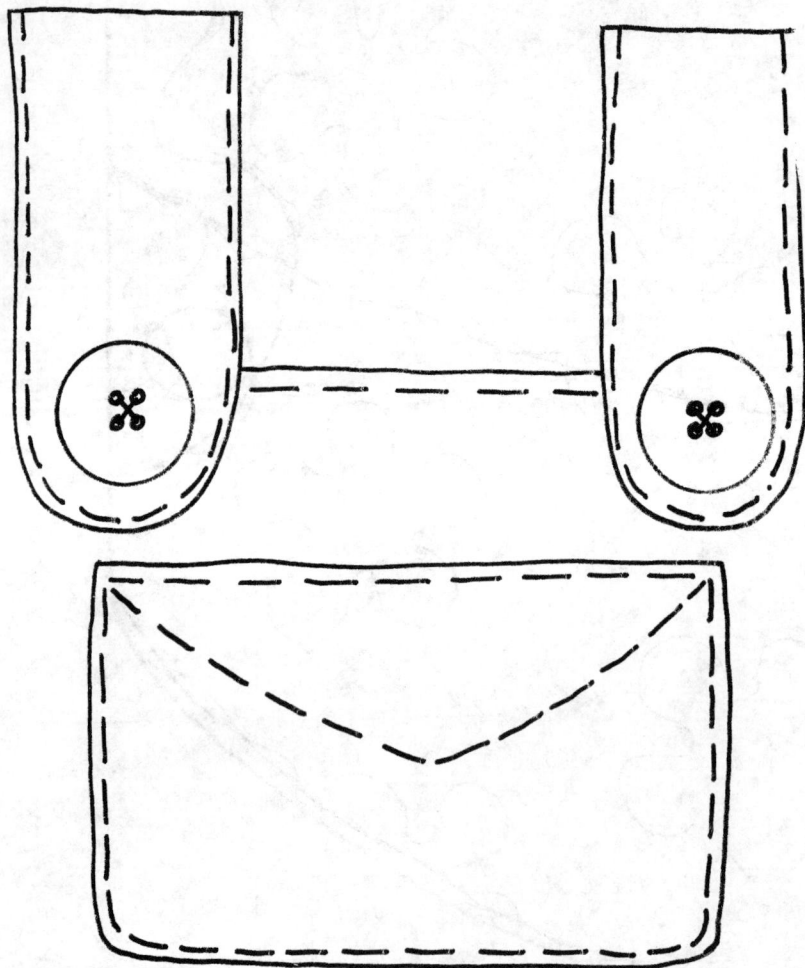

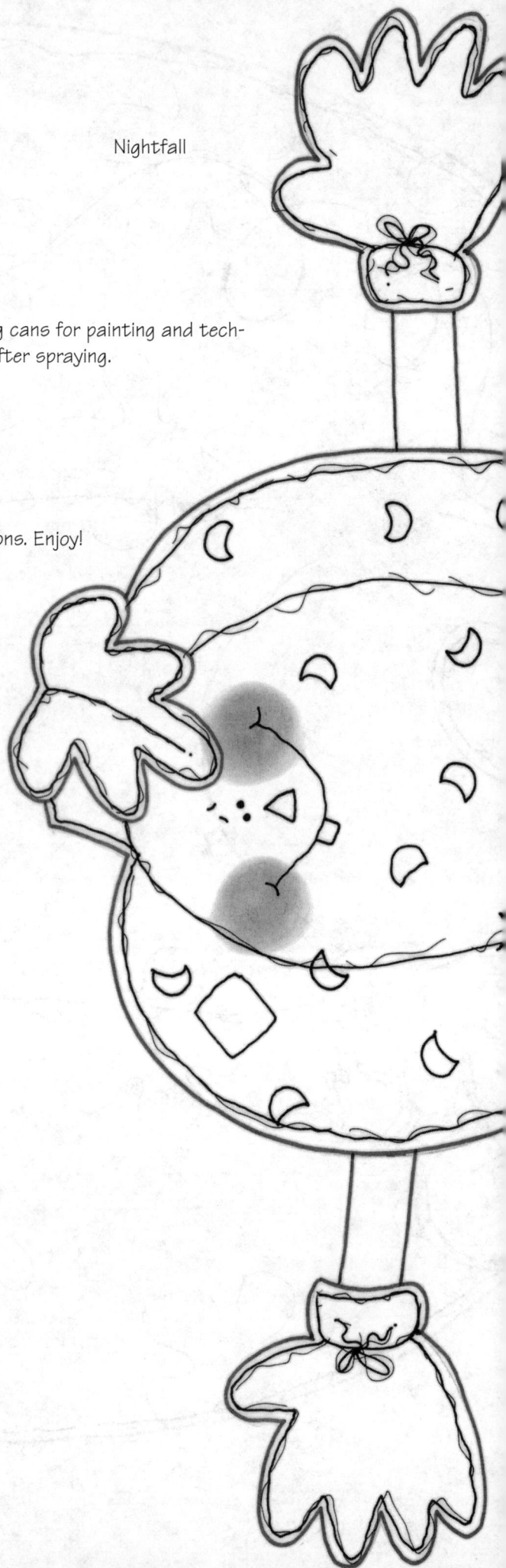

36

STANDING PUMPKIN AND SITTING PUMPKIN

This wood is not available through Provo Craft

PALETTE:

CERAMCOAT BY DELTA

Georgia Clay	Western Sunset Yellow	Liberty Blue	White
Apple Green	Leaf Green	Trail Tan	
Charcoal	Desert Sun Orange	Terra Cotta	
Cinnamon	Territorial Beige	Forest Green	

SUPPLIES:

Tan Paper Twist Two Pieces 3 1/2" long
Mini Black Pom Pom
HeatnBond
Two 5/8" Axle Caps
Two New Pencils (with new erasers to cut moon and cross shapes for stamping)

Black Pearl Cotton
Fabric Scraps (for patches)

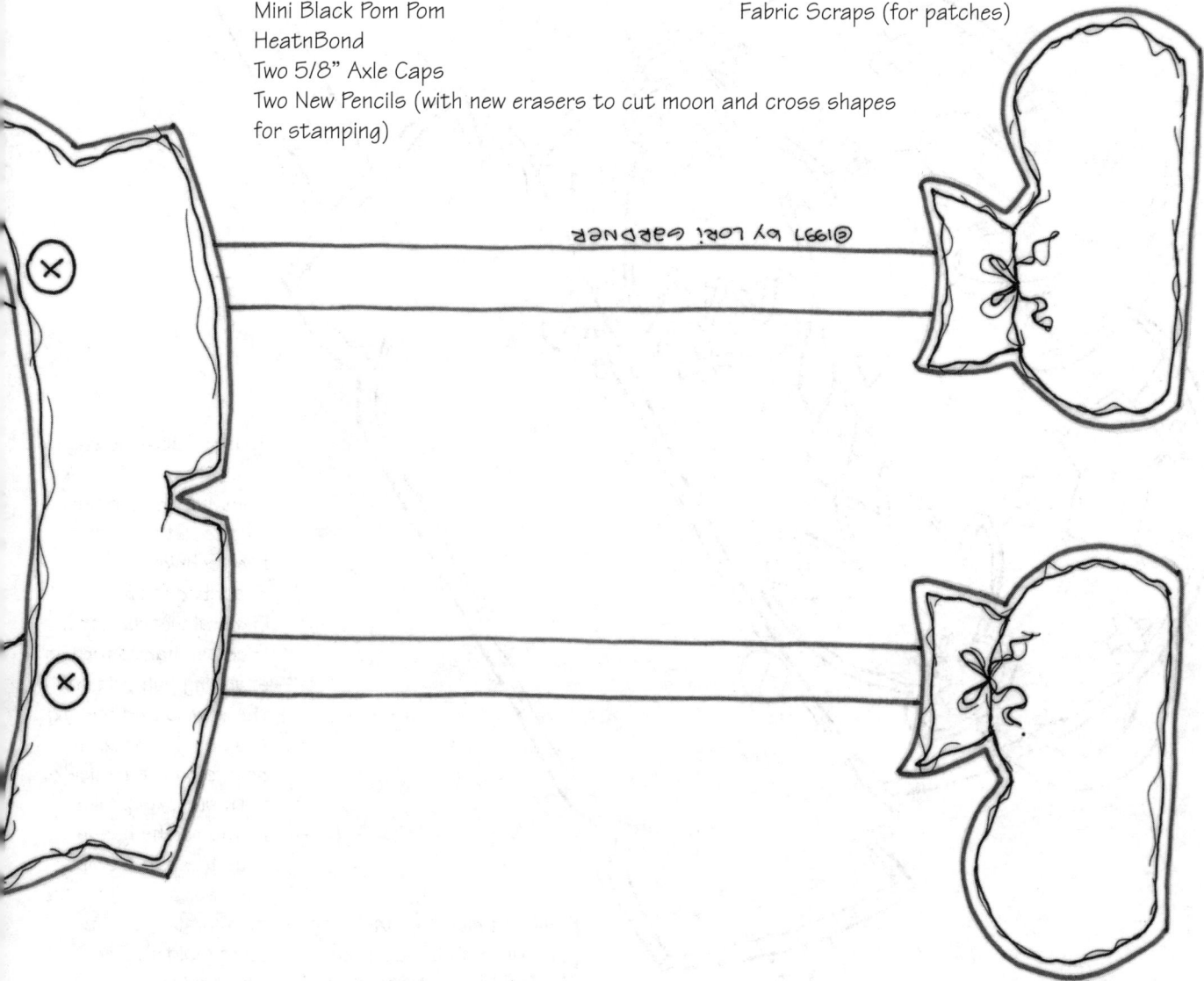

©1997 by LORI GARDNER

WOOD CUTTING HINTS: Body, hands and shoes are cut from 3/4" pine. Leaves are cut from 1/4" pine. Two dowels are 1/2" x 5 1/2" for the standing pumpkin's legs. Two dowels are 1/2" x 2" for the arms on the standing pumpkin . Two dowels are 1/2" x 2 1/2" for the legs on the sitting pumpkin. The overall finished size for the standing pumpkin is 11" x 10 1/2". The sitting pumpkin is 5" x 11 1/2".

PAINTING INSTRUCTIONS:
1. Terra Cotta: Base in the pumpkins.
2. Liberty Blue: Base in the shorts.
3. Territorial Beige: Base in the shoes.
4. Trail Tan: Base in the hands.
5. Apple Green: Base in the dowels.

6. Leaf Green: Base in the leaves.
7. Charcoal: Base in axle caps (spider body). Dot the eyes.
8. Desert Sun Orange: Stamp the cross shapes onto the sitting pumpkin.
9. Western Sunset Yellow: Stamp the moons onto the standing pumpkin. Dot buttons on the shorts.
10. White: Base in the tooth on the standing pumpkin.
11. Cinnamon: Base in the noses on both pumpkins and tongue on the sitting pumpkin. Dry brush the cheeks on the faces.
12. Georgia Clay: Wash in the mouth on the sitting pumpkin.
13. Forest Green: Base the stems.

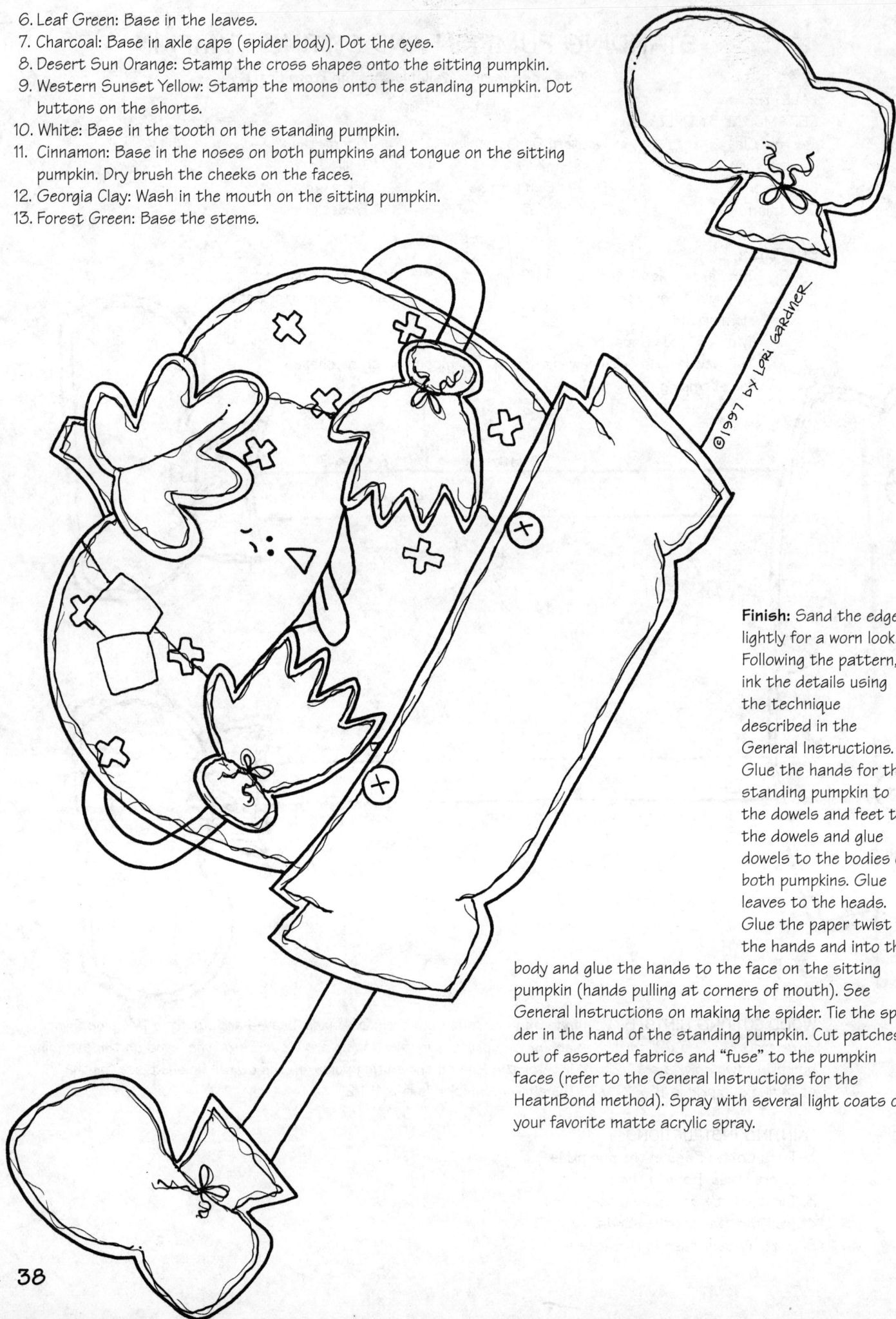

Finish: Sand the edges lightly for a worn look. Following the pattern, ink the details using the technique described in the General Instructions. Glue the hands for the standing pumpkin to the dowels and feet to the dowels and glue dowels to the bodies of both pumpkins. Glue leaves to the heads. Glue the paper twist to the hands and into the body and glue the hands to the face on the sitting pumpkin (hands pulling at corners of mouth). See General Instructions on making the spider. Tie the spider in the hand of the standing pumpkin. Cut patches out of assorted fabrics and "fuse" to the pumpkin faces (refer to the General Instructions for the HeatnBond method). Spray with several light coats of your favorite matte acrylic spray.

©1997 by LORI GARDNER